Robert Pace

CREATIVE MUSIC

1. Play as written, then for creative reading, try inverting the patterns or beginning on the middle note. Transpose to Db and Eb major.

2. Find a repetition and a sequence, then transpose to d and f minor. Also, invert patterns for creative reading.

1. Improvise both *parallel* and *contrasting* answers for this question. Then, after a few days, create new melodic questions over this same bass pattern.

Question

2. After creating both *parallel* and *contrasting* answers the first day, make up new questions and answers each day. Change the notes but keep the same rhythm.

Question

3. Notice the *parallel* and *contrary* motion in this question. You may change this as you make up your own new questions in this same style.

Question   **Answer**

4. Experiment with *block, off-beat* and *Alberti* bass patterns for this question and answer. Also, change it from major to minor mode.

Question   **Answer**

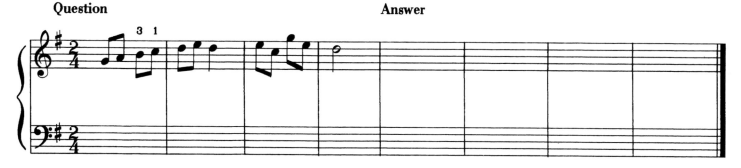

1. Observe all phrasing and dynamic markings as you play this. Transpose on alternate days to E and C major.

2. This example uses only major triads, with the exception of the d minor triad in the left hand. After playing as written, transpose down one whole step.

1. Complete the last two bars of this question, then improvise both *parallel* and *contrasting* answers.

Question

2. Improvise at least three *contrasting* answers each day for this *bi-chordal* question. Also create your own *bi-chordal* questions with appropriate answers.

Question   **Answer**

3. Make up several *contrasting* answers each day to this *whole tone* question.

Question

4. Include the *ii chord* in your answers and transpose to F and A major.

Question

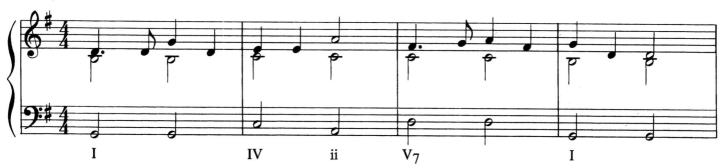

German Dance

1. Play the first time as written, then repeat for some creative reading. Also, transpose to A and A♭ major.

HAYDN

Sonatina

2. Transpose to B, D♭ and D major.

CLEMENTI

1. Improvise both *parallel* and *contrasting* answers each day, then write one answer in the blank staves below.

Question

Answer

2 Make up *contrasting answers* using extended scale line as found in the question. Also, create new questions using this same chord pattern.

Question

3. Keep the *ostinato* pattern in the left hand and use the *blues scale* in the right hand to improvise new questions and answers.

1. Try to scan the treble and bass clefs at the same time to see both the general contour and any specific patterns (such as sequences, repetitions, inversions, etc.) Transpose to G and A major.

2. Compare this example with "Gigue," MP page 9, to see the similarities and differences. After playing this as written, you may make further changes for some creative reading.

3. For creative reading activities, you may change from *parallel* to *contrary* motion (or vice versa) and invert patterns. Transpose to D and Db major.

1. These two questions are related to "Menuett" (MP page 9). Improvise *parallel* and *contrasting* answers to each one and transpose to the keys of F and A major.

a. **Question**

b. **Question**

2. This question is related to "Gigue" (MP page 9). Begin your answer with two sixteenth notes on the last beat in the fourth measure. Make up both parallel and contrasting answers.

Question

3. After creating both parallel and contrasting answers to this question, work out new questions with *ascending scales* in the first and third measures. Tranpose to Db, Eb and E major and be sure to check your scale fingerings for each new key.

Question

1. This example presents the following fingering problems:
   a. Finger substitution (changing from one finger to another on the same note, as in the first measure).
   b. Crossing a finger over the thumb (measures 2 and 3).
   c. Contracting the hand by using the thumb then 5th finger, as in measure 7.
   Transpose to C and E major.

2. Notice the sequential patterns as you read this example, then change them slightly for some creative reading.
   Transpose to Eb and Db major.

JOHANN HÄSSLER

Allegretto

1. Make up both parallel and contrasting answers using *diatonic triads* with the *chord root on top.* Also improvise new questions in the same style.

Question

2. In your answers, continue to harmonize the melody with the Alberti bass pattern as in the question. Then experiment with new questions and answers.

Question

3. For the first few days, create several contrasting answers for this question. Then as it becomes easier, improvise new melodies over the bass pattern. Transpose to D, Db and E major.

Question

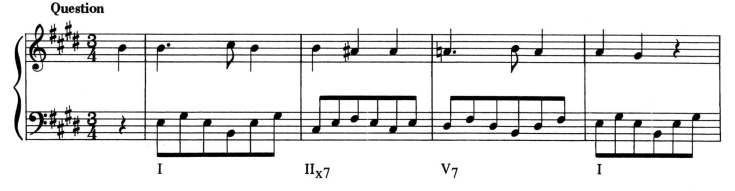

4. Make up both parallel and contrasting answers in the style of the question. Transpose to A and B major.

Question

1. Play as written, then change the rhythm for practice in creative reading.

2. After playing this several times as written, let the right hand take the lead and the left hand follow.

1. Sharps and flats may be interchanged in the *row* (compare this with MP IV, page 12).

Row

2. Look at the row (above) as you make up new answers for this question. When you want to move through the row more quickly, avoid repeated notes and patterns or long notes.

Question   **Answer**

3. Write your own row or *series* using these 12 chromatic tones in a new order. Avoid more than two consecutive tones (half-steps) from the chromatic scale without making a skip or changing direction.

Chromatic Scale

Row

4. Use your new row to create your own questions and answers.

Question

1. Using appropriate fingering in playing double notes is very important, therefore some fingering has been supplied at crucial points. *Glide* from one key to the next when using the thumb on two consecutive notes, as in the first measure. Also shift the fingers quickly in the fifth measure when crossing the 5th finger over the 4th. Transpose to D and E♭ major.

2. The last two measures of each of these phrases moves more than the first two, therefore it is important to select a good fingering for them before you begin to play. Transpose to B and B♭ major.

DITTERSDORF

1. Improvise both parallel and contrasting answers to this question, then make up other questions and answers using *double notes* in the right hand.

Question

2. Use *suspensions, passing* and *neighbor tones* in your answers to this question, then create new questions in the same style.

3. Make up contrasting answers to this *whole tone* question. Also, put the melody in the bass with *tone clusters* in the *right hand*.

Question

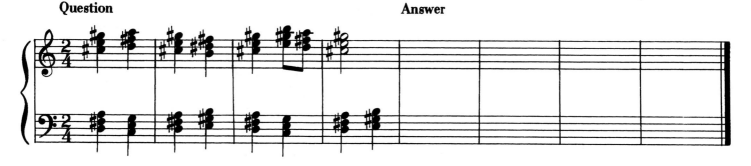

4. After improvising both parallel and contrasting answers to this *bichordal* question, notate one answer in the blank measures.

Question   **Answer**

1. Transpose to the keys of f and g minor.

2. Play as written, then do some creative reading by adding *passing* and *neighbor* tones. Transpose to A♭ and G
   major.

1. Create both parallel and contrasting answers to this question, then make up your own questions in the *Lydian mode.*

Question

2. Use this question as a beginning for creating other questions and their answers in *Phrygian mode*.

Question

3. This question is in *Dorian mode* (half steps between the 2nd-3rd and 6th-7th degrees of the scale). Improvise questions and their answers here, then move everything down one step in G Dorian and make up others.

Question   **Answer**

4. Relate the melody tones in the right hand to the *quartal chords* in the left hand as you create answers to this question.

Question   **Answer**

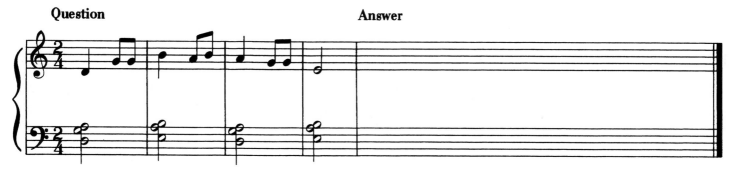

1. First, play this as written, then do some creative reading by inverting patterns and changing the melodic direction.

F. CHOPIN, Op. 68, No. 2

2. Again, try your creative reading skills on this piece after playing as written.

SCHUMANN

1. Plan your answer before playing the question. Also create new questions using this same rhythmic pattern.

Question

2. Use *diatonic triads* in your right hand for answers to this question.

Question

3. Refer to *Jazz Is A Way of Playing*, page 7, for more ideas on developing these call and response patterns using the blues scale.

a.

b.

1. Play as written then transpose to f and e minor.

2. Transpose to F and A major. See *Tricks With Triads*, Set 2, for other examples of diatonic triad movement.

3. Notice which voices move and which remain on the same tone. Transpose to E, E♭ and F♯ major.

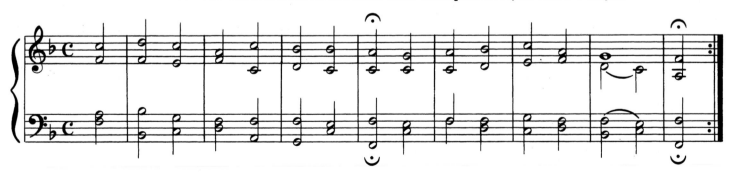

1. Here are the beginnings for two questions which you may extend for another four bars. After creating parallel and contrasting answers for these questions, make up other questions with the chords in the same position (root on top).

a. **Question**

b. **Question**

2. Write your own question with the triads in any of their three possible positions, then create both paralllel and contrasting answers.

3. In this question, the chords appear with the 3rd on top. Create contrasting answers over these chords.

Question

1. Before playing this, notice that while the two voices are moving in the same direction, the lower voice has more skips and may be more difficult to read. Try some creative reading and transpose to G and A major.

2. There are many possibilities for creative reading in this example. Transpose to D♭ and E♭ major.

1. Play this variant of the first phrase of "Quadrille" and improvise several answers. Then make up your own questions based on this same piece and give both parallel and contrasting answers.

Question

2. Use this example to get ideas for other variations on "The Chase." Let one hand imitate the other or use contrary motion as at the end.

3. Work out the patterns for your answer (sequences, repetitions, inversions, etc.) before you begin to play the question.

1. After playing this as written, read creatively by changing the direction of the lines in either hand and/or adding embellishing tones (upper and lower neighbors, passing tones, etc.). Transpose to F major.

2. Identify each chord in this chorale excerpt. Notice that the vi7 in the third measure and the ii7 in the seventh measure appear in their first inversions. Transpose to D and Db major.

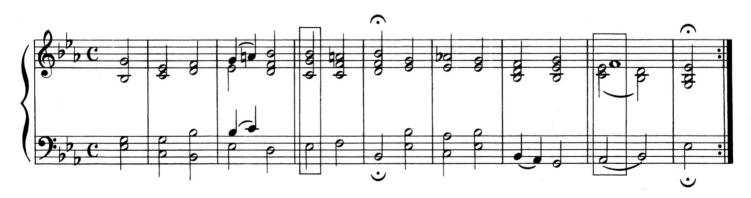

1. Improvise parallel and contrasting answers with passing tones, lower and upper neighbors, and perhaps an *appogiatura*, as on the first beat of measure four.

Question

2. Make up both questions and answers using chord tones from these 7th chords. Transpose to D major.

Question   **Answer**

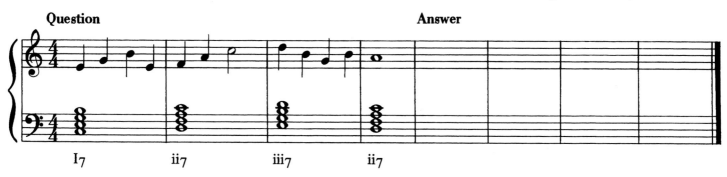

I_7 ii_7 iii_7 ii_7

3. Now use more stepwise melodic movement to create both parallel and contrasting answers. Also, make up new questions in this style.

Question

I_7 ii_7 iii_7 IV_7

4. Create both questions and answers in $\frac{5}{4}$ meter.

Question

1. Compare this example with "Sicilienne" to see where the melody and bass parts have been altered. After playing as written, try some creative reading and transpose to g minor.

2. Invert the melodic patterns but keep the same harmony in the left hand for your creative reading. Transpose to a and f minor.

1. Make up several contrasting answers to this question, then still using the same rhythms, create new questions and their answers.

Question

2. Improvise contrasting answers to this question, and make up other questions over this on similar 7th chord patterns.

Question　　　　　　　　　　　　　　　　　　**Answer**

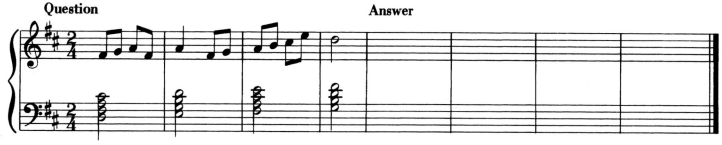

3. Improvise parallel and contrasting answers using the II_{x7}, then create new questions on this same harmonic pattern.

Question　　　　　　　　　　　　　　　　　　**Answer**

I　　　　　　II_{x7}　　　V_7　　　　I

4. Use this question as a model for improvising other questions (and their answers) in *Phrygian mode.*

Question

1. Work out the fingering for this example, then write a few finger numbers on the score to help you remember them.

2. Listen to the *bichordal* sound of this example and notice that both first and second inversion triads are used in the right hand while only triads in the root position are used in the left hand. Play as written, then do creative reading and transpose to F major.

1. Improvise contrasting answers to this question, then keep the rhythm of the left hand and create new questions and answers.

Question

2. Make up answers to this *bichordal* question. Create your own questions and answers in this same style.

Question   **Answer**

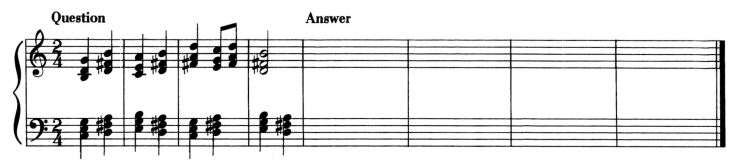

3. After improvising answers to this question, change the meter to $\frac{4}{4}$ and use an Alberti or off-beat bass accompaniment for your own questions and answers.

Question   **Answer**

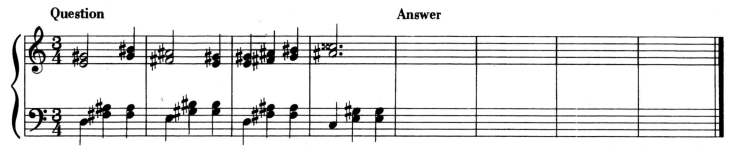

4. Improvise contrasting answers over these 7th chords and transpose to G major.

Question   **Answer**

1. Study the patterns of notes to work out your best fingering. Invert some of these patterns for creative reading.

Sonatina

CLEMENTI

Allegro di molto

2. Write in your fingering in places where you need to put the thumb under, a finger across, or substitute fingers. Transpose to F major.

Sonatina

KÜHLAU

Allegretto

2332

1. Make up a parallel answer to this question, improvise a new question with its answer, then return to the first question and answer. This will give you a Three-part-form (ABA).

Question

2. Improvising a two-bar "response" to the "call" will give you a four-bar phrase. Keep the same chord pattern and improvise new melodies.

Call   **Response**

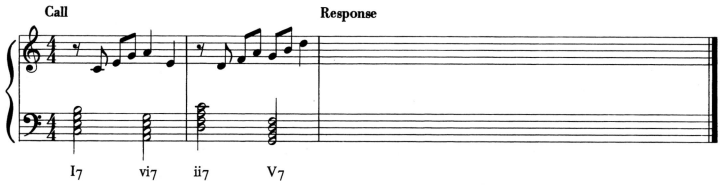

I_7 vi_7 ii_7 V_7

3. Create new questions with neighbor tones, chord tones or repeated tones.

Question   **Answer**

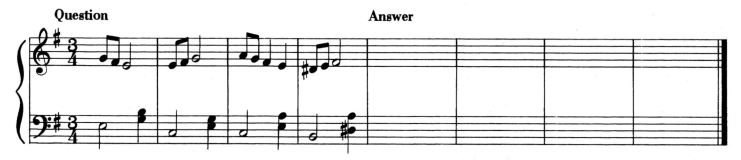

4. Notice the sequence and repetition in this question. As you prepare your answer and make up new questions, be sure to decide *before* you begin which patterns you want to use. Transpose to E♭, D and F major.

Question   **Answer**

1. Study the similarities and differences between this example and the first eight bars of "Rondeau," MP page 32. Mark the fingering at certain strategic places to remind you when to put the thumb under or a finger over the thumb. Transpose to D♭ and C major.

2. In the Baroque period, musicians would embellish the musical line with passing tones, upper and lower neighbors, etc. For example, in the first measure, you could fill in the interval of a third with a passing tone. Try embellishing either or both parts and transpose to A and G major.

1. Notice that this question has both contrary and parallel motion. Follow this same idea in your answers and other questions.

2. Work out your fingering patterns before you begin the question. Improvise both parallel and contrasting answers.

3. See how many different answers you can play for this question, then create new questions using the II_{x7} chord.

4. Make up and notate a question using this tone row, then improvise answers to it.

1. In the right hand, be sure to hold the dotted half notes while you play the other notes. Transpose to G and F major.

GRIEG

2. Play as written, then transpose to F, Gb and Ab major. Be sure to check your scale fingering before playing each key.

1. Improvise contrasting answers using mainly 3rds and 6ths in the right hand. Also create new questions in the same style.

Question

2. Use the II_{x7} in your answers to this question, then make up other questions with the same harmonic progression.

Question

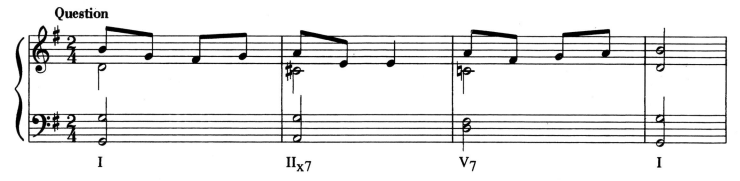

3. Create other questions with contrasting answers, having the melody move back and forth between right and left hands.

Question

4. Analyze these quartal chords to see the spacing and doubling of tones. Improvise new questions with appropriate answers.

Question

1. Make these quartal chords very legato. After playing as written, transpose up and down one whole step.

2. The bass pattern here is similar to the third measure of "Suite For Piano." Keep the same bass but change some of the melody notes for creative reading.

3. Transpose to B, E♭ and E major.

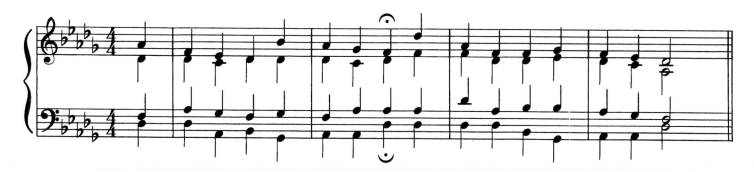

1. Improvise contrasting answers to this question, then make up new *quartal* questions.

Question   **Answer**

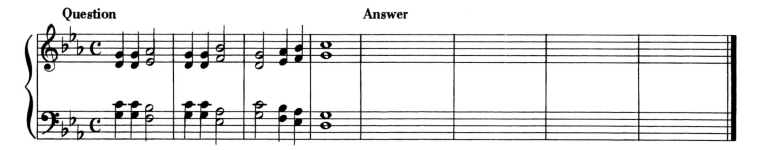

2. Create other *bichordal* questions, both on this rhythm and others of your choice.

Question

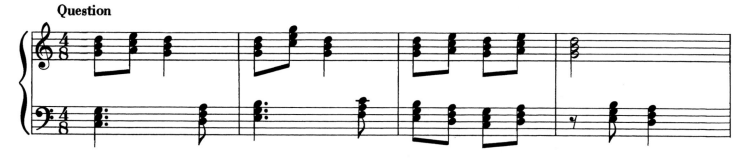

3. Notice that the 7th chords in the bass have the 5th omitted. This is done to keep the bass from becoming too "muddy" or heavy sounding. Make up many questions and answers on this chord progression.

Question

I₇   vi₇   ii₇   V₇

4. Improvise contrasting answers then create other *linear* questions.

Question

Sonatina

1. The bass pattern in the Sonatina is typical of the classical period. Keep the same harmonic structure but change the upper part for some creative reading.

KŪHLAU, Op. 55, No. 1

2. Work out the appropriate scale fingerings as you transpose this example first to A♭ and B♭ major, then to G and B major.

2332

1. Make up contrasting answers to this question, then create new questions in the same style.

Question

2. Give parallel answers to this question, then create new questions using the iii chord.

Question

3. Create contrasting answers using either ascending or descending scale patterns.

4. Give both parallel and contrasting answers to this question and transpose to d minor.

1. Study the patterns in both parts to see whether the line moves by skips or steps. Change the patterns for your creative reading and transpose to F and A major.

Allegro

2. First play as written, then make a few changes each day for creative reading. Transpose to D♭ and E♭ major.

C.P.E. BACH

Andantino

1. Improvise both parallel and contrasting answers for this question.

Question

2. Make up an answer for this question, then improvise another question and answer for a "B section." You may also return to the original question and answer to complete an ABA form. Transpose to d and e minor.

Question   **Answer**

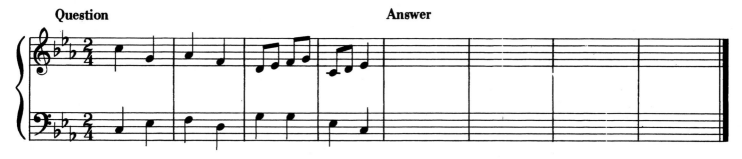

3. Create both parallel and contrasting pentatonic answers.

Question

4. After making up answers to this question, improvise other melodies over a similar bass pattern.

Question

German Dance

1. Before playing this piece, analyze the harmonic structure to see the relationship between right and left hands. For creative reading, change only a few notes of the melody.

SCHUBERT

2. Play as written, then transpose to A and G major.

From: Six German Dances

SCHUBERT

1. First create contrasting answers to this question, then make up other questions and answers in the same style.

Question

2. Again, after creating contrasting answers, improvise new questions and answers in the same style.

Question

3. Improvise other questions and answers over this same chord progression.

Question

I_7 vi_7 ii_7 V_7

4. Use this bass pattern to create questions and answers using the *blues scale*.

Question

1. Observe the phrasing carefully. Transpose to E and F major.

2. Play as written then make a few changes in the melody for creative reading. Transpose to a and e minor.

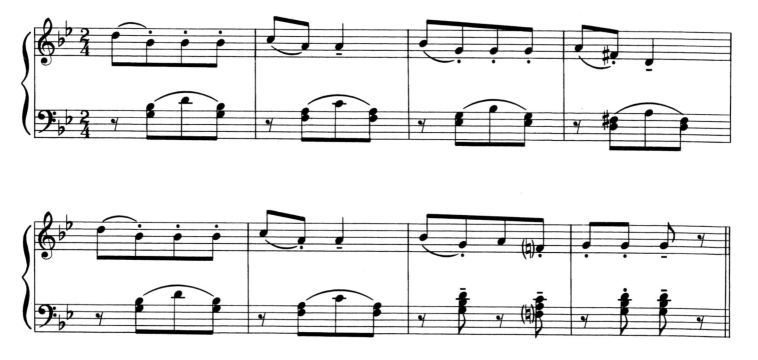

1. Make up answers to this question then create new questions and answers with the melody in the left hand.

Question

2. Create both contrasting answers to this question and new questions and answers in the same style.

Question

3. Using this same *linear style*, improvise new questions and answers in minor mode.

Question

4. Use this question as a model for creating other questions where the bass has 7th chords moving by steps.

Question   **Answer**

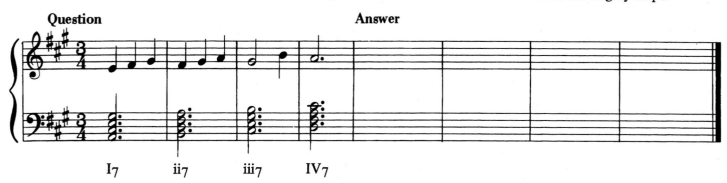

I₇   ii₇   iii₇   IV₇

1. Observe all phrasings and dynamics as you play this. Avoid looking at your hands where they skip from one position to another.

Allegro

BEETHOVEN, Op. 33, No. 2

2. Each time before playing this, look for harmonic, melodic and rhythmic patterns.

Allegretto 1

BEETHOVEN, Op. 33, No. 3

1. Make up contrasting answers to this question, then create others in the same style.

Question

2. Use this question as a model to create other questions and answers in *Lydian mode*. You can think of the Lydian mode as a major scale with a raised 4th degree.

Question

3. Improvise other bi-chordal questions and answers on any bass pattern and with any other rhythm.

Question

4. Combine chord tones with scale line in your answers. Create similar questions and answers in other keys.

Question